Places Around Town

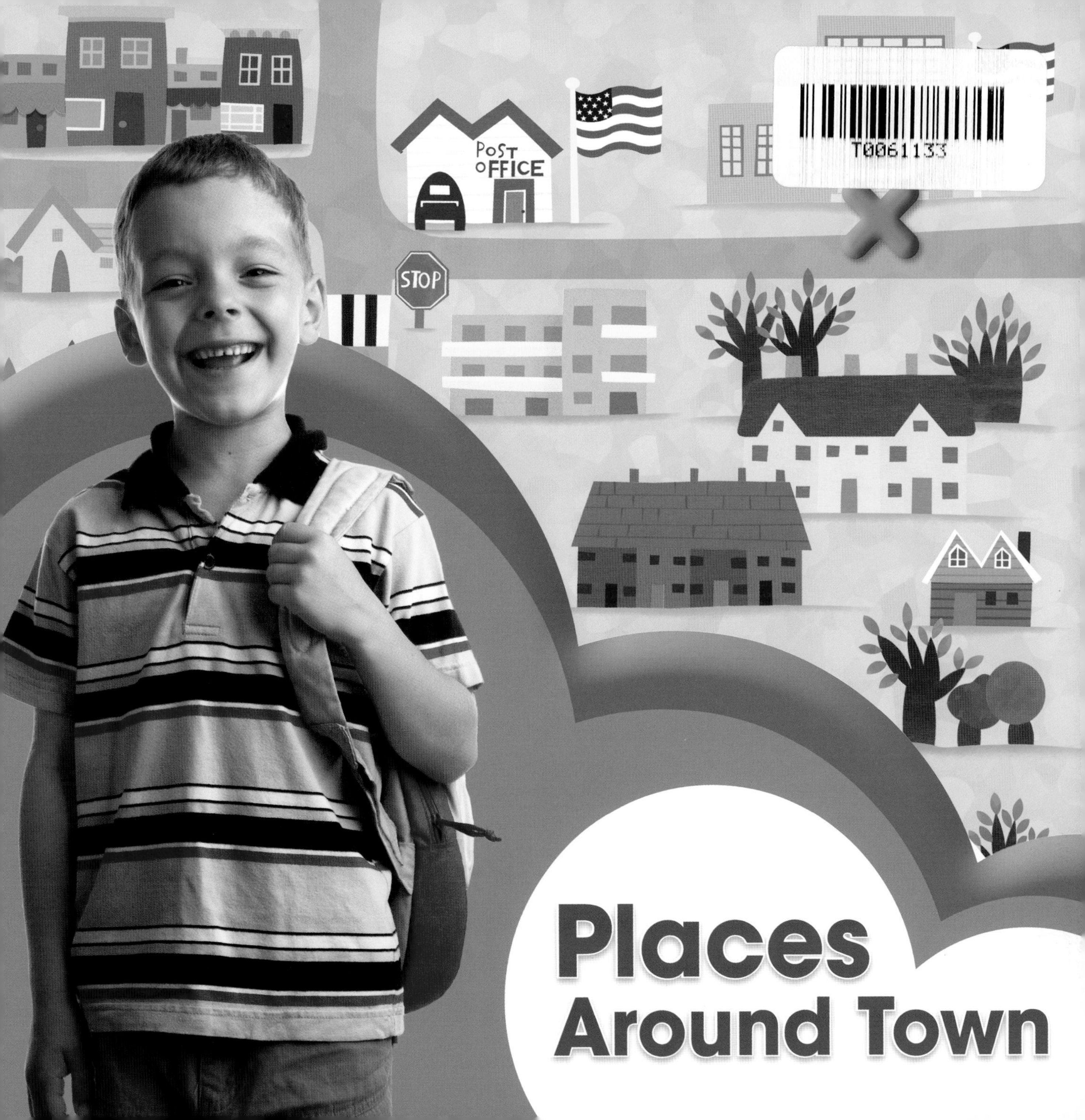

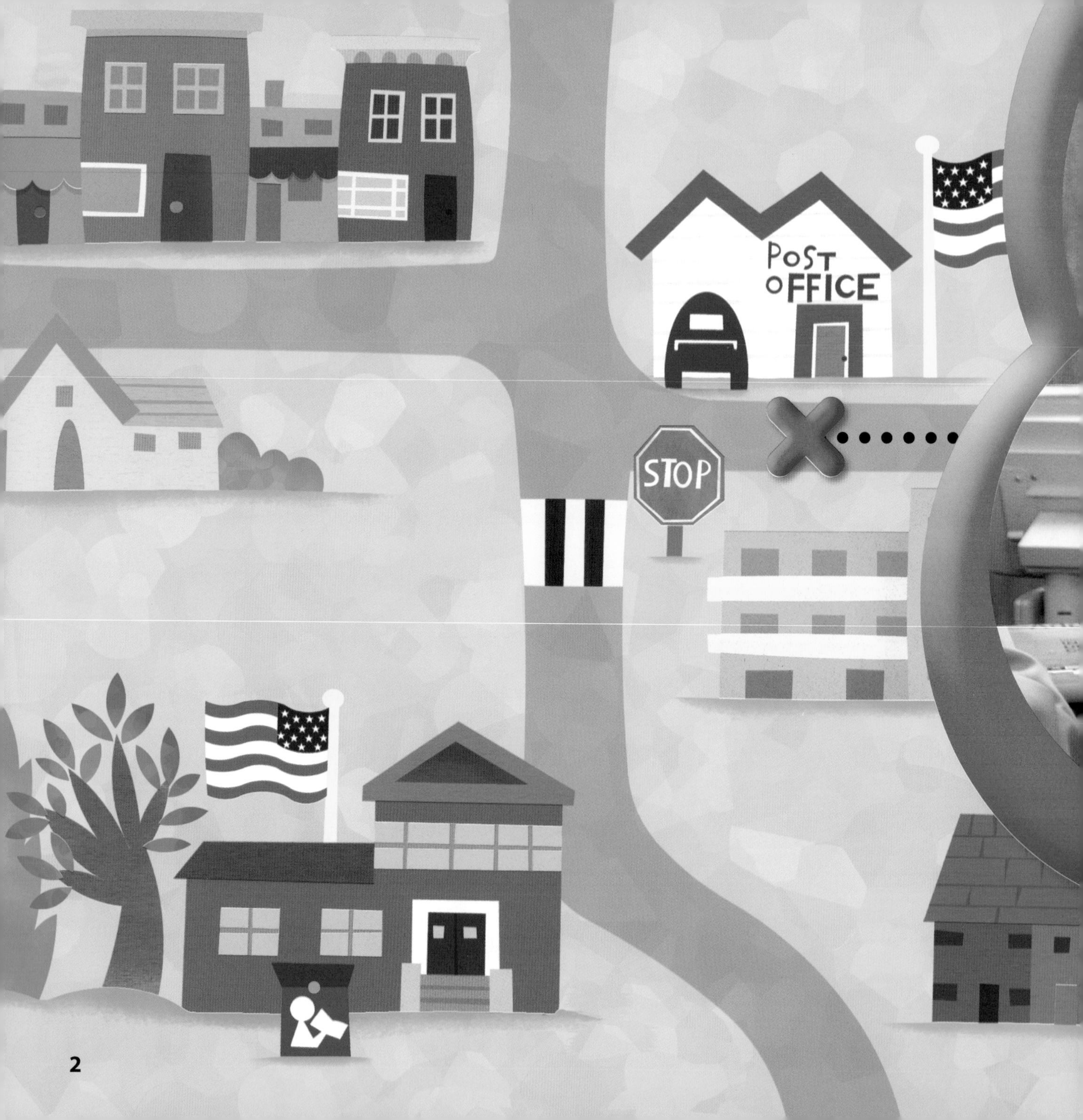
POST
OFFICE
STOP

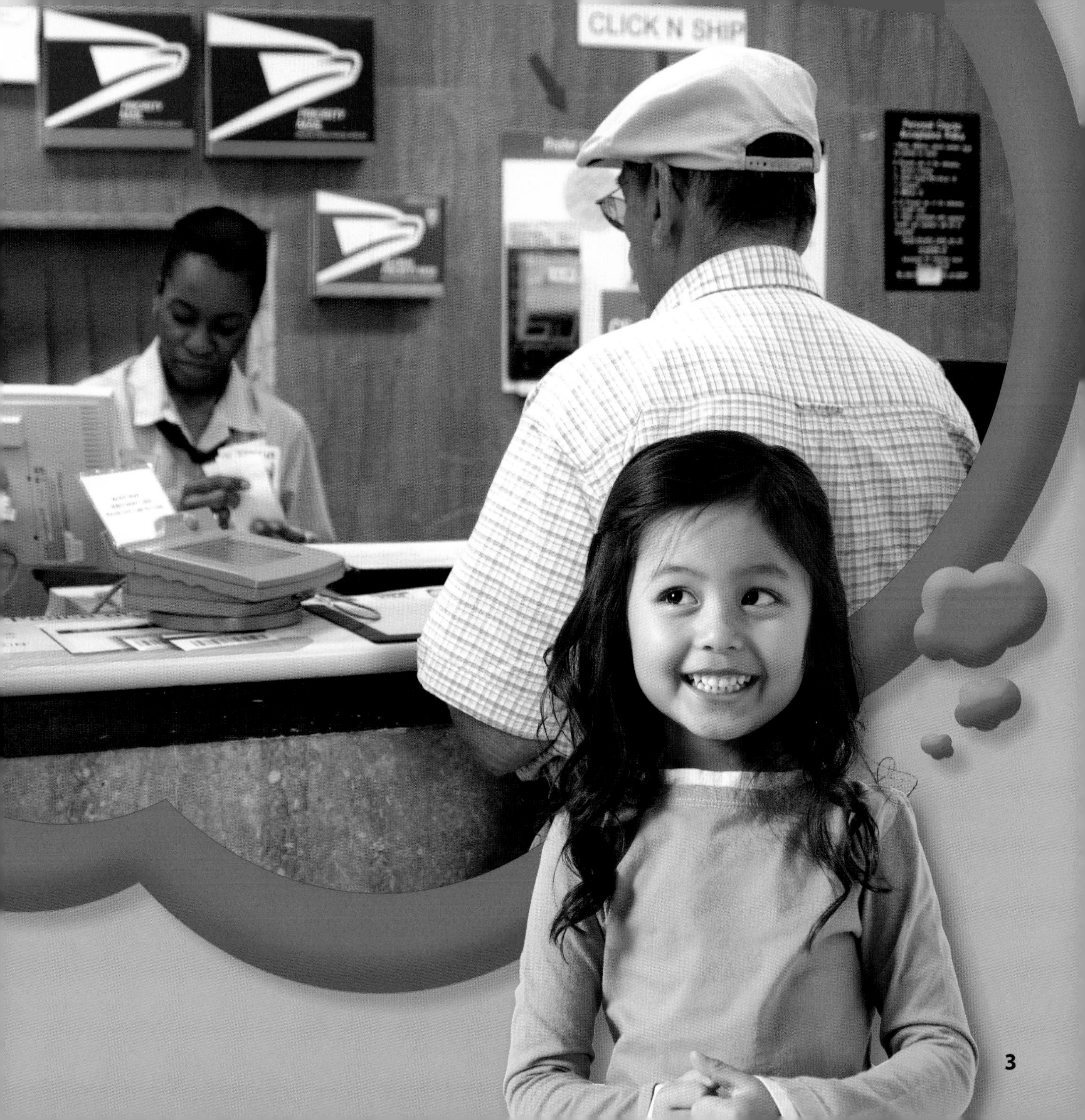
CLICK N SHIP

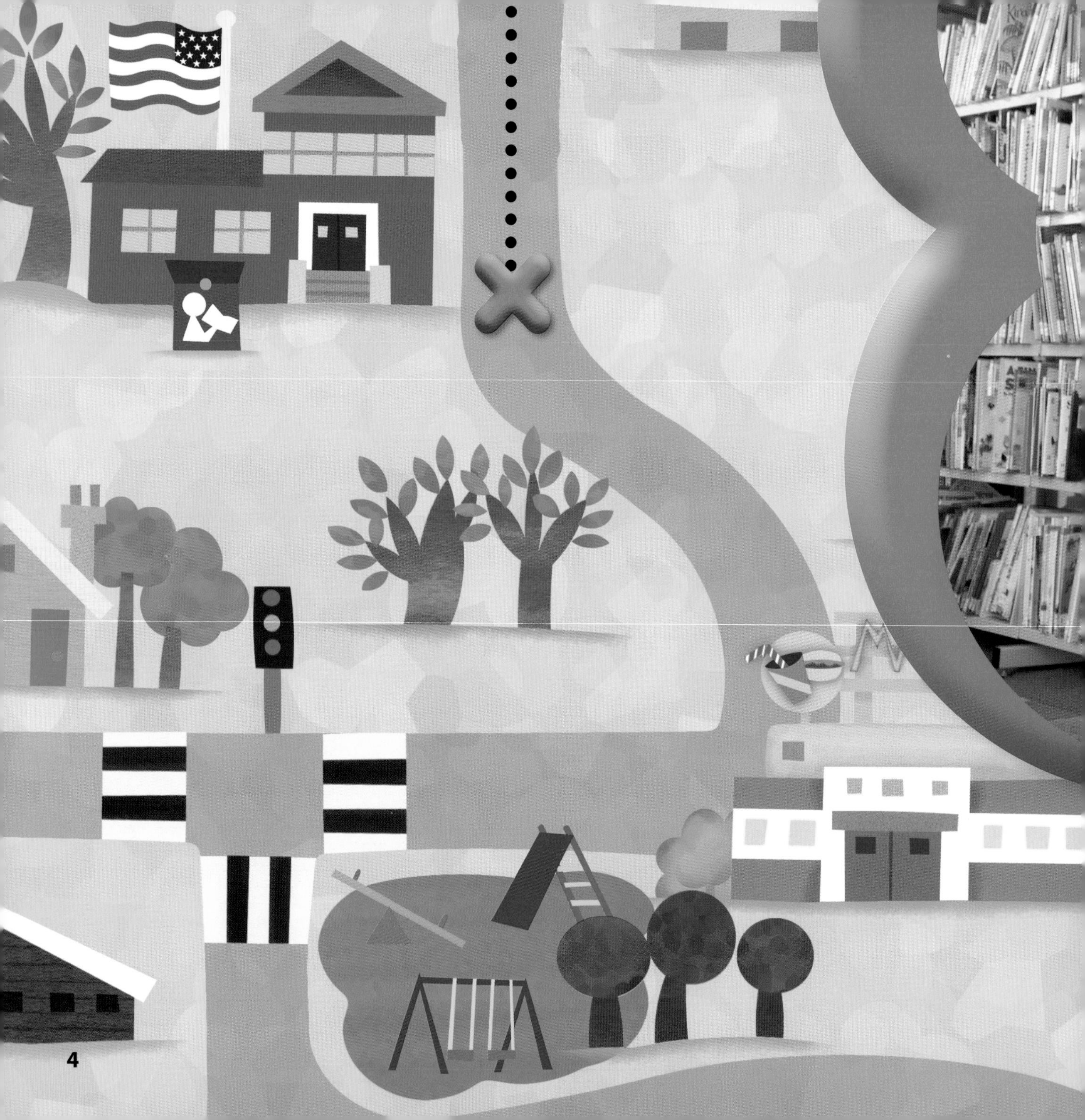

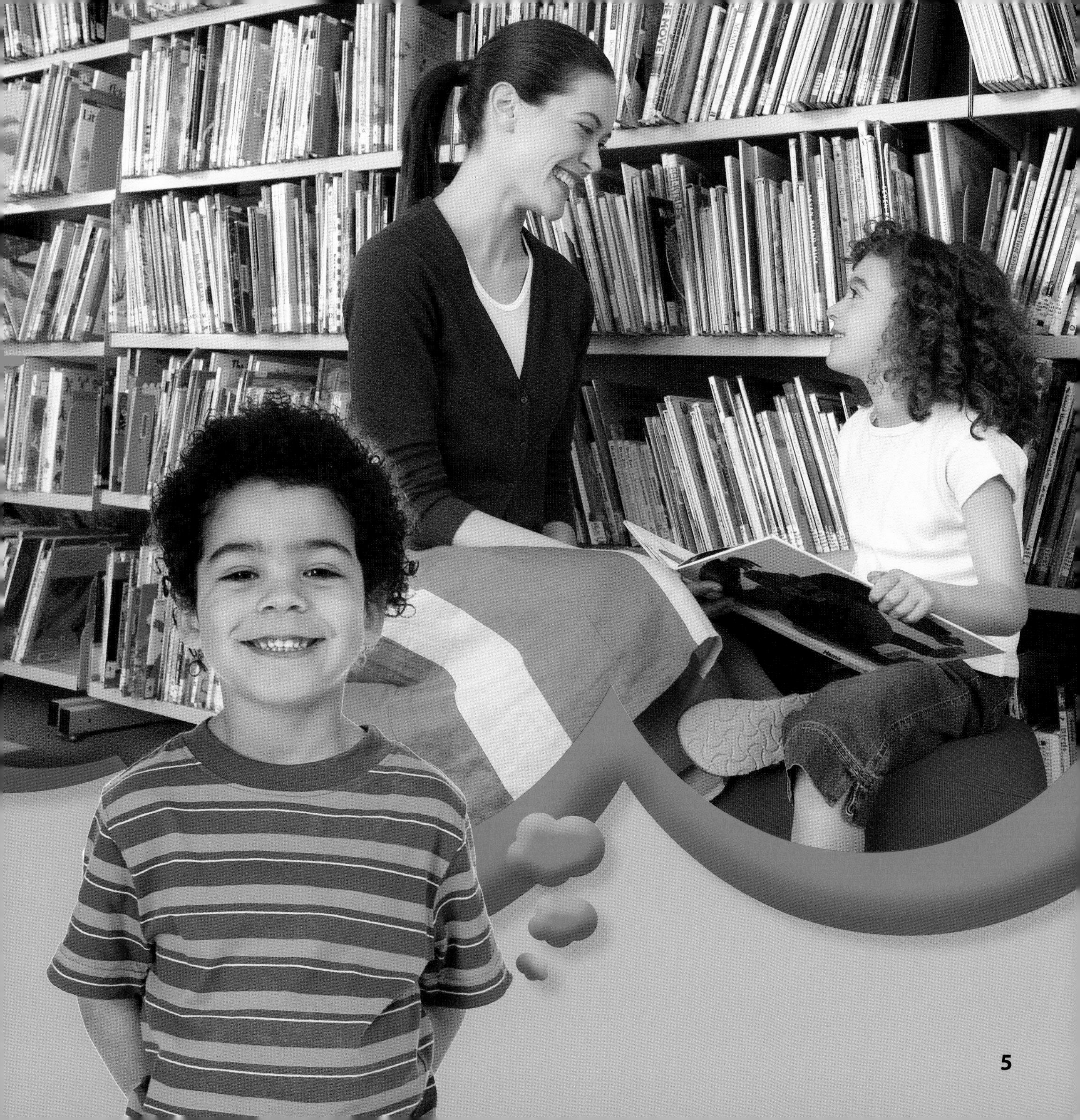

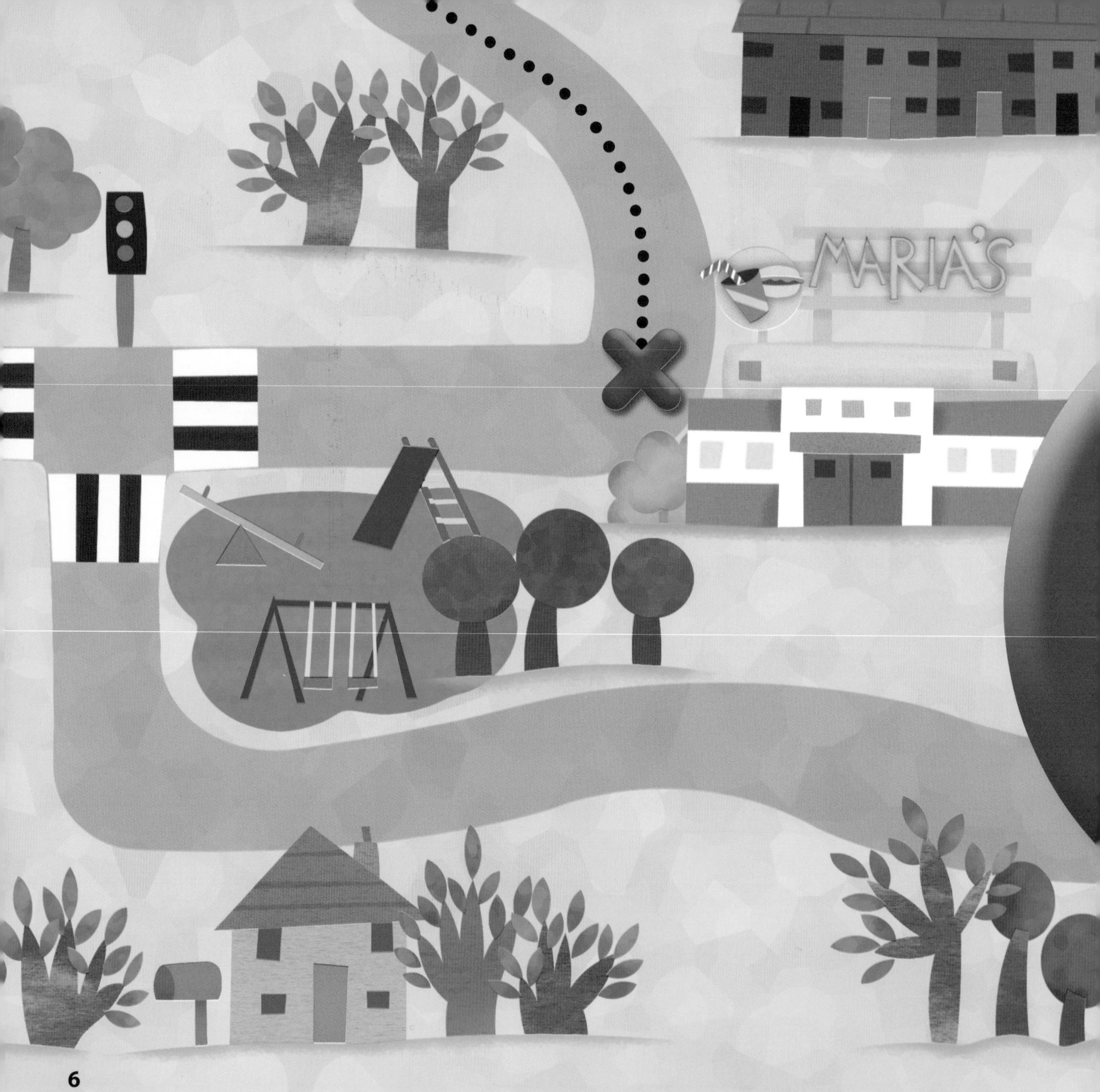
MARIA'S

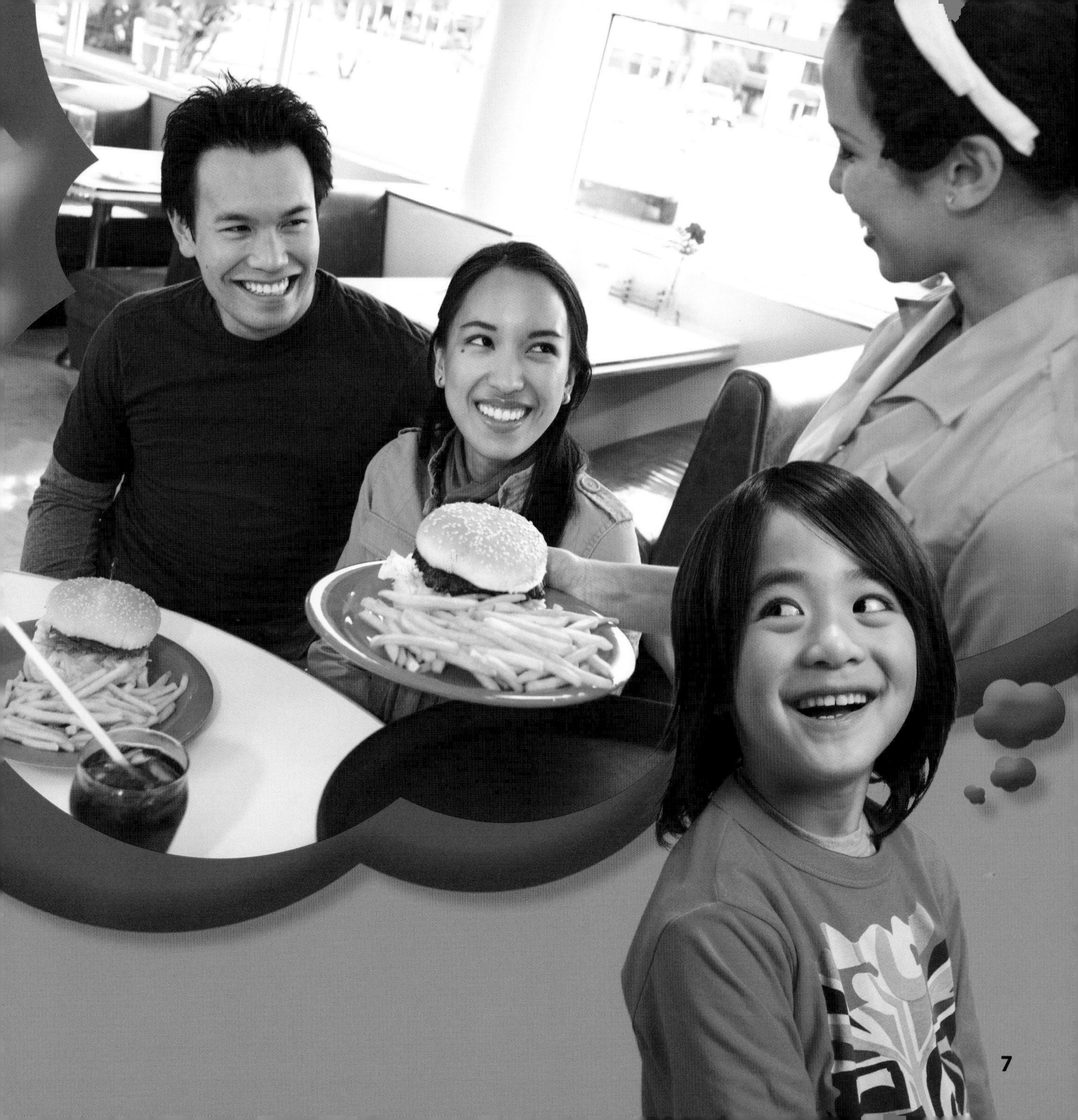

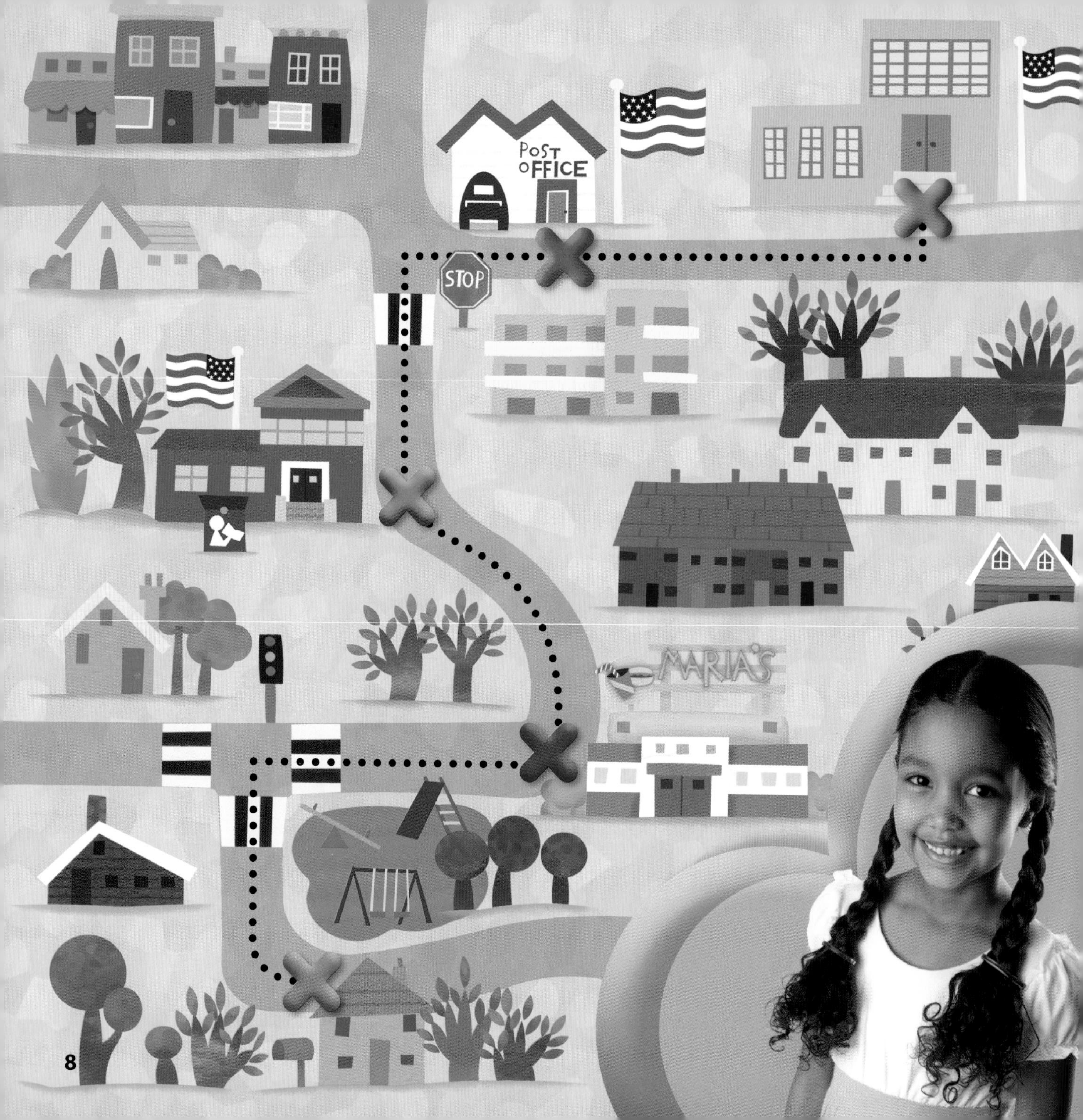
POST OFFICE
STOP
MARIA'S